Abby Buchanan Longstreet

Cards;

Their significance and proper uses, as governed by the usages of New York

society

Abby Buchanan Longstreet

Cards;
Their significance and proper uses, as governed by the usages of New York society

ISBN/EAN: 9783337714758

Printed in Europe, USA, Canada, Australia, Japan

Cover: Foto ©ninafisch / pixelio.de

More available books at **www.hansebooks.com**

GOOD FORM

CARDS

THEIR SIGNIFICANCE AND PROPER USES

AS GOVERNED BY THE USAGES OF NEW YORK SOCIETY

BY THE AUTHOR OF "SOCIAL ETIQUETTE OF NEW YORK"

NEW YORK
FREDERICK A. STOKES & BROTHER
MDCCCLXXXIX

CONTENTS.

CARDS.

VISITING CARDS: THEIR SIGNIFICANCE AND STYLE.

WHENEVER personal interviews are difficult or impossible to arrange, cards are the most convenient and direct means of social intercommunication. Their correct style and appropriate uses are a recommendation for a stranger, while an inelegant card, or an untimely or mistaken employment of it, is hostile to a chance of friendship between such as have little or no knowledge of each other. Indeed, an unrefined card, or a misuse of one, is a trial to the tempers of most persons with cultivated tastes, even though its bearer possesses recognized virtues.

Its appearance and its appropriateness to the occasion testify to its bearer's or receiver's familiarity or unfamiliarity with approved usages, though its inelegance may be in defiance of them. Whether it is ignorance, or an intentional neglect of accepted etiquette, the result is unfortunate.

Its tint, texture and engraving are also witnesses to its owner's habits or to his knowledge of the most approved customs in the social world, which evidence is seldom untrustworthy.

If it were not that a presentation of a visiting card conveyed more information regarding unknown persons, habitual associations, also their measure of social culture, than their clothing and manners, less emphasis would be placed upon the value of its style and usage. Raiment may be a local or a transitory fashion, and manners a momentary, rather than a customary grace and graciousness, while a visiting card, though a trifle in itself, is seldom other than personal and characteristic.

A conformity to what may be called the timely uses of cards, indicates a delicate considerateness of such customs as the best society has approved and adopted. Their appearance, added to their reasonableness, is an announcement to modern society not unlike that which was conveyed by a ring in ancient times. Its bearer was then at once recognized and placed above or below the salt at a nobleman's banquet. To-day the card may not seat its bearer where he would like to be placed, but its misuse, or its ill appearance, is likely to deprive him of an opportunity to secure what he desires.

The significance of a card, and especially its convenience, is not unconsidered and unappreciated by very busy men and women. It is a communication in

cipher, expressing a pleasure or a sorrow of one's own,
or a quick human sympathy with the griefs or gladness
of others. Its fitness to the occasion is not only a
touching congratulation, or a tender condolence, but,
as has been intimated, its fashioning, and the hour of its
presentation, are an explanation of much of its owner's
individuality. Its simple and elegant lettering or its
showy, eccentric, or in any wise peculiar engraving,
an exaggerated or diminutive size, a fanciful hue, or
an ornamental ink, brings with it to a fastidious
stranger, a satisfaction or an unpleasant repelling sensation that it is difficult if not impossible to forget.

Society may be frivolous or inconsiderate in many
things, but underlying its vanities there are strata
which have an excellent reason for being, and the
etiquette of cards is one of them. A written name
implies that its bearer's formal cards are temporarily
exhausted, or are beyond reach, and if neatly and
plainly inscribed, it is acceptable; but an engraved *fac-
simile* upon a visiting card is an evidence of its owner's
egotism or conceit, and it bars the way to the best
social recognitions, unless he or she has strong forces
outside of themselves to aid them in making desirable
acquaintances. Such an intrusion of personality as
one's own fashion in penmanship made permanent by
engraving, is decidedly offensive to those who have
reserved natures and exclusive social positions. Ap-
parent egotisms are incompatible with perfect breeding.

A correct card is white, but not intensely white. It is fine in texture, not too heavy, or stiff, and in size it follows a prevailing mode. An exaggeration of the usual shape is bad form.

MEN'S CARDS.

THE visiting cards of men are slightly shorter and much narrower than those at present approved for women, because upon the latter informal announcements are sometimes to be written, and upon a man's card none are likely to be required. The latter is engraved in slightly larger text than the former, and is a plain script without flourishes or ornamentation of any kind. Certain occupations, or rather professions, may properly be denoted upon a man's card. It should indicate his rank in the army or navy, and should be engraved in full before his surname, or in abbreviation with his complete name, and changed with his promotions; otherwise it might not only be inconvenient but very embarrassing to those who make presentations to him, and also to a host when placing him at dinners and elsewhere.

The cards of such persons should be engraved thus:

5

General Peeble.

or,

Gen. John Gore Peeble.

101 *Fifth Avenue*

Col. H. D. Williams.

2 *Kilborn Street.*

or,

Col. Henry Ditson Williams.

2 *Kilborn Street.*

It is approved style to engrave the titles of scholars and professional men, except Rev. before that of a clergyman, after the name. For example, Dr. as a prefix means many things. It may imply a complimentary or an earned rank. Indeed its significance is so varied that an abbreviated explanation following the name, such as M.D., D.D.S., LL.D., is least assuming and a more direct announcement of fact.

For social purposes it is quite as delicate and more fashionable to omit lettering indicating occupations, altogether.

All honorary titles, militia, political and judiciary, are strictly omitted from visiting cards, although it is not courteous or customary to drop them when addressing their owners by speech or in writing.

Where there is no indication of a title by a prefix or following an engraved name, the use of Mr. is invariable. If however he is compelled by any exigency to write his name upon a card, he omits Mr. and inscribes upon it his usual signature.

When his card is engraved, his address is placed upon the lower right-hand corner. If he is a bachelor and belongs to a club, the name of the latter may also be engraved, or be written upon the lower left-hand corner. If he lives wholly at a club, this residence is engraved in the right-hand corner of his card.

CARD ETIQUETTE FOR MEN.

NOT very long ago it would have been an impropriety, if not a rudeness, for a man to send a visiting card by post, except it were one with a bordering of black, which announced that its sender was temporarily neither visiting nor receiving. A change of usage became necessary because what is known as society is now so extended by members, and its obligations are so greatly enlarged, that facilities for meeting them become a necessity; therefore, etiquette consented that many social ceremonials be properly, though less elegantly, transacted by mail.

After-dinner calls by cards, calls of condolence, and a card after a first hospitality, whether the latter was accepted or declined, no matter how simple or informal such a courtesy was, must be left in person. If personal card-leaving is an impossibility, cards must be by messenger, with explanation by note.

Such calls of ceremony are obligatory within a week, and the earlier they are made the greater the respect expressed by the card or the visit.

9

Of course if the hostess has an "at home" day, and has indicated it upon her card of invitation or has mentioned it, it is imperative that he does not try to see her until that time. He may, and if she be entitled to especial respect, he should, call earlier at her door, to inquire for her health. He leaves his card with the attendant, but should not ask to see her. He cannot leave a card for her daughter or for any young unmarried woman in the house: but it is good form to leave one for the host, provided the latter's name was upon the invitation received, and not otherwise.

When he calls and sees his hostess but not the head of the house, he should leave a card for the latter on the hall table, or with a servant at the door. When for any especial reason, such as the presence of an honored guest in the house, many persons are calling at the same time, it is considerate to leave a card for both the hostess and her friend, as an assistance to the memory of those receiving.

On ordinary occasions, after the first call, leaving a card is an excess of formality and not in good form, if a hostess is at home.

ACKNOWLEDGING AN INVITATION TO A CHURCH WEDDING.

WHEN a man is invited to a church wedding and cannot attend, he must send his card or cards in an envelope directed to those who invited him. If the invitation was issued in two names, he responds to both names upon the envelope in which he sends two cards by mail or by messenger on the day of the marriage.

If he is at the church, he leaves or sends his card or cards within a week, addressed to those who invited him. If they are strangers to him, and invited him because he is a friend to the groom, cards, and by no means a call, should be a response. To do more than this might be considered an intrusion.

11

AFTER MEN'S ENTERTAINMENTS.

WHEN a man entertains in a formal manner, each man invited, whether present or not, calls in person, leaves a card, or sends one by post, or writes a note of thanks within a week. This civility is obligatory. To omit it is not only an ingratitude, but such negligence of a customary courtesy may be understood to mean that he who fails of such politeness is ignorant of good form or is contemptuous of the customs prevailing in well-bred circles. If it is known that he is familiar with established etiquette and fails to respect it, he is pronounced insolent and is not likely to be invited again.

CARDS DECLINING TO CALL IN THE AFTERNOON.

A MAN cannot leave his card upon a lady even after a pleasant acquaintance with her at parties and elsewhere, unless she has intimated that he may; and only married or elderly women in well-bred circles are likely to say, "I am at home on such or such days between four and six."

When it is said, it is equivalent to a formal invitation, which cannot, in courtesy, be ignored. A man may feel compelled to reply that his occupations are pressing and that visits in the afternoon are quite impossible, and he will express a regret at declining. Instead of a call at the time mentioned, he should send his card by messenger on her first "at home day" during her receiving hours. If her husband is an elderly man, or is an invalid, he directs the envelope to both, and encloses two cards.

13

MEN'S VISITS TO EACH OTHER BY CARD.

VERY little card-leaving is in vogue between men, but certain ceremonials cannot be omitted, especially if the acquaintance is a recent one. Of course, if a man is not at home a card is left for him by a visitor. If there has been a change of residence a card announcing it is left at the door, or is sent by mail.

Men who have been introduced to each other and expressed cordiality, or who have a common interest in each other's pursuits, have less difficult and formal methods of becoming known to each other than women.

A social equality recognized by both, a literary, artistic, or other achievement of either one or both, makes a call from one or the other not only possible, but natural, without an introduction, provided, of course, it is made when he who receives it is known to be habitually accessible to visitors. The caller, with or without an explanatory word regarding himself written upon it, may send in his card. If his visit is refused, it is obligatory on the part of the one

14

declining the visit to return a civil or kindly reason therefor, or appoint another occasion for a more timely call. Men seldom have as many, or as petty, excuses for declining an acquaintance as women; therefore for a man to refuse to see one of his own sex is rare, and such declination must have been reasonable. Hence there is seldom an unpleasant feeling left in the mind of the one whose presence has been refused.

Of course, an acquaintance may be desired by but one of the two men, in which case he who is visited may politely decline to see a stranger, or having admitted him, the call may be returned by a card enclosed in an envelope and sent by post. Of course, so ceremonious a return of a visit terminates all chance of an acquaintance that may have been opposed solely because of an over-busy life or perhaps an excess of visitors, which has become a burden to an occupied, but courteous person.

CARDS OF SYMPATHY.

AN unmarried man who has no near kinswoman to perform certain social duties that are obligatory in good society, is sometimes too negligent of them, and he wonders why it is he is so little regarded by those whom he really likes. If he would be made to understand that it is by small and prompt attentions which are spontaneously offered, more than by large displays of costly remembrances that friendship is won and retained, he might become more considerate. If an acquaintance is in sorrow, an immediate personal inquiry should be made, or a card should be sent by messenger. If distance makes this impracticable, then a card by the first post, touches hearts that do not forget if they have been shown sympathy when in grief or misfortune.

A card with congratulation written upon it, is sent to the father of the newly born, and to one whose engagement is just announced; also to the betrothed woman if she happens to be a friend, or a familiar acquaintance. Perhaps it is only a parent of a bride to be who is the friend, in which case " best wishes " may be written upon cards that are left or sent in an envelope, and addressed to both father and mother.

CALLING UPON A GUEST IN TOWN.

WHEN a man calls upon a woman who is a visitor in a family that is unknown to him, he must ask to see both hostess and guest, and send in a card for each. If his acquaintance is a young unmarried woman, it is obligatory upon the lady of the house to see the caller and remain with her. If the latter is not a young girl, the hostess need not come down until later, or, if declining to see the caller, she will, if a gentlewoman, send a kindly message with her refusal, and no man has a right to feel slighted.

A presentation to the hostess of his friend does not give him the privilege of a future acquaintance with her, or even a recognition from her, unless he is asked to call again, or is invited to partake of a hospitality. Whether he accepts or does not accept her invitation he must make a call upon her. If this attention is impossible before the departure of her guest, he can only leave a card at the door, except he has been distinctly invited by the host or hostess to continue an acquaintance. To call in his friend's absence without having been bidden to do so would be indelicate, and he might be suspected of that social crime, "pushing," but leaving his card is only a recognition of proffered or accepted hospitality.

He may prefer to terminate an acquaintance with his friend's hosts at once; but he cannot be discourteous to those who have entertained her, and proffered hospitality to him, because the motto of a thorough-bred man or woman is *noblesse oblige.* A card must be left, and left in person, and he must also make kindly inquiries regarding the health of his friend's late host and hostess. More than this he need not do, and less he cannot.

WOMEN'S VISITING CARDS.

MODERATELY large, nearly square, fine in their texture, thin, but not too flexible, and of a soft delicate white that is not intense in its clearness, are the prevailing characteristics of material for the visiting cards of women who respect good form.

Its engraving is script, not large, nor yet small, distinct, and with no ornamentation.

Usually a daughter's card is slightly smaller than that of her mother, but its style of lettering is the same. This diminution of form is, however, a matter of individual taste rather than an emphasized fashion.

It is imperative that Mrs. or Miss be placed before the name upon her engraved card. It is customary to use the husband's complete name, initials being less and less often seen upon visiting cards as the years go by. Except when a complete name is too large to be properly engraved upon a card of customary size, good taste omits initials and uses baptismal names.

The distinguishing convenience of an entire name

upon a card, except when the last one is uncommon, is very soon recognized in a city, and sometimes also in towns, if there are many family connections.

The oldest married woman in the oldest branch of the family may, if she chooses, omit baptismal names from her card, thus:

Mrs. Jamison,

10 *Elmwood Avenue.*

She, and she only, is entitled to this dignity and simplicity of form.

Unless a woman is elderly, she usually prefers the prefix of her husband's full name for all ceremonious or social intercommunications, or, at least, she prefers some part or parts of it. Since society is so extended and complex in its interests, an establishment of card usages, and the possession of an unmistakable name and an engraved address, are an immense convenience to overburdened memories. There is small chance of a social blunder being made with a card engraved thus :

Mrs. John Herbert Jamison,

Tuesdays.　　　　　　　　　　　　　　15 *Porter Place.*

A city or town is not added except in ink, and then only for use while away from home.

If a woman wishes to receive in a more formal manner than by a weekly "at home," or if she has a guest whom she wishes to introduce to her coterie of acquaintances, she may, for example, write the words *From three to six* above *Tuesday,* and the words *Jan. 10th* beneath *Tuesday.*

To shorten her season of receiving, it is etiquette to write under the engraved at home day, *Until Lent*, or she may limit the time to any date she pleases. Plates to be used year after year are properly engraved with the receiving month or months beneath the day of the week. This permits a pen to be drawn through the month not devoted to visitors. In the extension of social circles, women in New York are beginning to adopt the London and Paris custom of using cards with, for example,

First Tuesdays in
January, February and March.

on their left lower corner.

Such cards provide for absence from home and are most simple and convenient.

YOUNG WOMEN'S CARDS.

DURING a girl's first season in society her name is engraved upon her mother's card, as she has none of her own. She is appended as *Miss Jamison*, provided she is the eldest unmarried daughter of the eldest branch of her father's family, otherwise her full baptismal name is given with the prefix of Miss. Until she has been out one or two years it is not considered good form for her to pay or to make calls without her mother, therefore she requires no individual card. The mother's day and address, of course, serve for both.

In a family where there are unmarried aunts and cousins bearing the father's name, only one of all of them, and she the eldest unwed daughter of the eldest man, is entitled to the honor of using a card with *Miss Jamison* engraved upon it, although she may be the youngest girl by that name. By line of inheritance, she can, in justice, claim it.

When a second or third, or any succeeding daughter enters society, her name is added to her mother's card, and the sister preceding her has an individual one, but she uses also her mother's card when calling ceremoniously.

When two daughters enter society nearly together, it is customary for them to be mentioned upon their mother's card, thus :

Mrs. John Herbert Jamison,

The Misses Jamison,

Tuesdays.   10 *Porter Place.*

Of course this is customary only when they have a recognized right to such distinction.

If this honor belongs to a collateral branch, the full name of each daughter is engraved, the eldest, of course, preceding her sister.

When a mother has a receiving day mentioned upon

her card, her daughters at home, if unmarried, can use none upon theirs, nor can they appoint one formally in any manner, if their mother does not. It would not be respectful.

Until a girl is in society she makes visits within the family circle only, or with intimate family friends, and a card for her is needless.

INFANTS' CARDS.

IT is a recent and widening custom to announce the birth of a child by sending out a small card with its baptismal name in full upon it, also the date of its birth in the lower left-hand corner. It is enclosed in an envelope with its mother's card, the latter, of course, intimating that she is ready to receive visits of congratulation. A babe is the only untitled person whom etiquette permits a card that has not Mr., Mrs. or Miss upon it.

If visits are not possible, a card with *Congratulation* written upon the upper left corner is at once sent, addressed to the mother, promptness signifying a genuine sympathy with the happy parent. Those who are intimate send not only a card, but flowers, or a simple gift to the infant.

CARDS OF WIDOWS.

IF she chooses, a widow may, for social purposes only, continue to use the name she bore as a wife, custom permitting this usage simply because it is painful to erase a name that was given to a woman by one who is gone but is not forgotten. Etiquette overlooks such liberty, unless the widow has a married son who bears the same name as his father did, in which case he is no longer a junior, and the card that his mother prefers to keep, by right belongs to his wife. In such an instance the elder woman adds *Sr.* to her engraved name. If there are two widows having the same card, or claiming it, the younger one relieves the elder of an explanatory abbreviation by courteously adding *Jr.* to her own.

AFTER-MARRIAGE VISITING CARDS.

FOR use during the first year after marriage, it is proper, but not *de rigueur*, that a visiting card be engraved thus:

Mr. and Mrs. John Herbert Jamison,

Tuesdays.   *15 Porter Place.*

A reason for this is that it is supposed that all first after-marriage calls are returned by husband and wife together. Of course each has his and her individual card for other purposes, but a combined one, even though it is to be used by the wife alone, is understood to signify that the visiting *convenances* of the first year of wedlock are respected.

Afterwards, when the wife attends to her husband's social duties, as most wives must, this card is not used; but it is an appropriate and convenient one to send with wedding and other gifts that are presented by both. It is also in good form when making inquiries for the sick; it is a fitting messenger to afflicted acquaintances with whom one is not sufficiently intimate to write a note, or to whom one is not entitled to send flowers. It may be left or sent by either, or be carried by both, as a condolence or congratulation.

Whenever it is impossible for a newly made husband to return first calls during the formal receiving hours of his own or his wife's friends and acquaintances, this combined card, if left in person by the wife, is accepted as a returned call; but it is not a custom to use it for ceremonious calls, after the first bridal round of visits is completed.

CARDS OF NEW ACQUAINTANCE.

An unmistakably older woman, an invalid, or one who is professionally occupied with literary or artistic work, or one who is recognized as an active philanthropist, may send her card to a younger or less occupied woman, if, having been introduced to her, she wishes to meet her again. The latter responds in person within ten days. If the sender of the card has an "at home" day and it is indicated by the card, this date is the only one on which a first call can properly be made.

Two women must indeed be very friendly, in fact, intimate, if they call upon each other at another time than on a receiving day when there is one.

If the receiver of a first card cannot increase the number of her acquaintances, or the sender is an undesirable person to know, or social attractions have not been mutual, a card may be sent or left in return at the first proper moment, and no personal visit need be made. Many a woman with a long visiting list, or one who is habitually busy, looks upon an added acquaintance as an increase of social burdens that are already beyond proper management.

Such refusals to establish a visiting acquaintance are sure to be softened in some kindly and well-bred manner. The reason may be so frankly explained, or at least some one of several reasons, the tenderest, of course, being selected, and the courtesy of the explanation so genuine, that the pain of the denial is charmed away. A real regret always underlies a necessarily inflicted wound, and the one who is hurt recognizes it, if at all delicate of feeling, or sensitive to unexpressed reasons.

CARDS OF WOMEN FOR, AND AT, AFTERNOON TEAS AND RECEPTIONS.

An afternoon tea cancels many small obligations and opens a not very difficult way by which kindly responses may be made to overtures for a more intimate acquaintance that must be denied. Cards for a simple afternoon tea should be sent a week or ten days in advance of the date upon them. A visiting card is used, and words such as *Tea at four* are engraved or written over the fixed day or under the name, and the date in the month, thus, *Jan. 10th*, is written or engraved beneath the day of the week.

Tea cards may be sent by post or by messenger, according to convenience, and they require no reply. This sort of tea is only an opportunity for one's acquaintances to pay a visit to the hostess *en masse*, and such hospitality is counted as a call made upon each guest and the reverse. Those who cannot be present send their cards on this afternoon, and thus they also have cancelled a social debt.

Those who are present, both men and women, leave

their cards in the hall or place them in the hand of a servant who announces them.

A circle may be so large that two or three teas are given to divisions of acquaintances and friends, and a clever hostess is she who knows how to arrange this discreetly.

It may not be amiss to mention that a kindly guest, and certainly a well-bred one, will not make such groupings a distress to her entertainer. The latter cannot always know the private likes, and the small personal aversions of her acquaintances. To do a right thing wrong is an unpleasant blunder.

If invited men cannot be present at an afternoon reception, and few can, a wife, sister, mother, or some kinswoman may leave their cards for them as she goes out. If there is no announcing by name, she may leave them in the hall with her own card as she enters; but the ceremonial of having a man mention each guest's name as she enters a drawing-room, is becoming more and more common. If a man has no recognized relative who has the care of his visiting obligations, he sends a card by post or messenger on the afternoon of the receiving day.

If the host receives with the hostess, or even if the invitation included his name, and he does not receive, an invited man sends two cards, but if he is present, he leaves but one, a second deposited card being a lately renounced foolishness.

There may be a daughter's name upon the hostess'

card of invitation, but it has no recognition by the cards of guests, if she be a young girl. If she is unmistakably past her youth, it is courteous to post, or to leave, a man's card for her also.

When an entertainer invites friends to assist her in receiving, it is customary for the hostess to propose to those who are to thus assist her that she be permitted to invite, also, a few of the acquaintances of the latter. If this suggestion is an agreeable one, the visiting card of each assistant is placed in the hostess' envelope and sent out. These guests are presented to the hostess, or are announced, and cordially welcomed, and the etiquette of leaving their cards, or of sending them, if the invitation cannot be accepted, is just the same as if they were friends of the hostess. This ceremonial demands no after courtesy, or recognition of social indebtedness to their entertainer. The call or the sending of cards under such circumstances is an attention due only to the one who assists at the tea.

If a mutual regard is recognized at this introduction, mutual requests for a continuance of an acquaintance are an easy and natural matter that settles itself. No one is wounded if there is no recognizable fitness in a continued knowledge of each other.

Usually, of course, those who are to receive with an entertainer try to select for invitations such of their friends as are likely to be sympathetic,—persons whom they hope she will be pleased to add to her list of visitors; but of such a result no one can be assured, so subtle and so blindly instinctive, as well as so unreasoning, are likes and dislikes. It is foolish, while the world is so full of all sorts of people, for any one to waste his or her moral, and perhaps vital, energies in striving to overcome a distaste for the personality of a stranger, who, most likely, has no need of her, and doubtless feels a similar distaste. It may be a feeble repulsion that one woman has, but if it is thorough enough to be an unmistakable or positive sensation, it is more than likely that the other one would feel the same if she were not too much absorbed to be conscious of it at the moment. Such instinctive oppositions may afterwards be effaced, and perhaps be forgotten if they were vague, but in large and constantly widening circles of society they may as well serve as protectors against ponderous visiting lists.

CALLING CARDS AND THEIR PRESENT USAGES.

THERE was a time when a card was folded over at the right side, and left with a servant to assure the one called upon that it was brought in person. Such cards of others as came by the same hand, and whose senders were supposed to be unable to call, were not folded over. The left side of each of the cards was then folded over to signify that each person in the family was included in this attention. This custom, happily, has fallen into disuse, except one is leaving cards upon some elderly person, and wishes to be deferential to such as cling to the usages that prevailed in their prime. It had serious inconveniences, because, in order to make clear such a pantomime of cards, they were much crumpled, and became far from elegant in appearance, even though, according to a prevailing usage, they were orderly in their wrinkles.

Afterward there was a time—but happily a brief one —when it was held to be *en règle* for a woman caller to leave a card for herself upon each one of her sex whom she visited in the family. If she was married, she left her husband's cards also, and perhaps, also, the cards of other male relatives, upon each of the same women, and also upon every man in the house, even if there were half a score of sons and nephews. It was fortunate for those times (though the same custom still prevails in certain localities) that etiquette did not demand that cards should also be left upon young unmarried women, else would the accumulation of Bristol board, also the quantities to be carried about from house to house, have been more absurdly exaggerated than they were.

Preposterous as was this short-lived fashion, it remained in vogue long enough for its remembrance to perplex many persons who are not habitually in society, but who wish to be correct, and are bewildered by memories of what was once called the etiquette of cards. Happily, the brief custom of invading or showering a house with visiting cards has been relegated to that mysterious place where our dropped follies sleep. It is hoped that this place of storage is not overcrowded. It needs much spaciousness, because there are other follies of custom, not mentionable at present, that will doubtless be retired to it before the end of this century.

It is the present vogue in good society, and most likely it is permanent etiquette, for a lady who calls and does not see the one whom she had hoped to find at home, simply to leave her card. If it is at a hotel, she pencils, for example :

For

Mrs. James Henry Brown,

on the upper left-hand corner of the front of her card. If Mrs. Brown is at a private residence, an unmarked card is left for her with the servant. It is not good form to leave a card when calling upon a resident except there has been a change of address, provided the visitor sees the person for whom the call is intended. Sometimes, if the attendant is new to the place and does not seem to be quick of comprehension, and the call is not on "at home" day, it may be discreet to send in a card. If the person called upon is engaged or out, the caller leaves her own card and two of her husband's, one for the mistress and one for the master of the house. If she sees the mistress, and there is no reason for reminding her by a card that they have met, she leaves only the cards of her husband, father or brothers, according to her setting in life.

This formality is due once at the beginning of each season, except after a formal entertainment, when, as has been explained, the cards of men who were guests, or who declined invitations to be such, are left at an early date.

Exceptional reasons only excuse unmarried sons from doing their own card duties. When this is impossible, their cards are left at the same time as their father's and by the same hands. In London after-dinner cards are left next day. This alacrity is said to be prompted by a kindly desire to ask after the health of a hostess, who, presumably, has fatigued herself in an unselfish desire to give pleasure to her guests. Cards of the entire family are sent by post after a change of residence, also after returning from a prolonged absence in Europe or elsewhere. After an ordinary summer away, this ceremony is properly omitted, except by young society men, who are expected to leave cards or call as soon as they are back in town, or as early as their friends have returned home again. When leaving for a long absence, and there is no leisure for paying *congé* visits, cards with *p. p. c.* written in their lower left-hand corners are sent by post. This is an imperative custom. It is usual also when leaving a summer or winter resort. It is a recognition of courtesies, and it furnishes an opportunity for leaving one's address. It also spares one a formal leave-taking. It is equivalent to saying, " If you choose to remember me, when we meet again we can take up agreeable associations without that formality which is necessary between those who but lately were strangers to each other." This is all that *p. p. c.* means when written on cards left for guests one has met only at hotels or after an agreeable *camaraderie* of travel.

CARD ETIQUETTE FOR WOMEN INVITED TO WEDDINGS IN CHURCH.

THE sending of cards, if one is invited to the church only, also of after-cards when one has been present at the house, or when invited to the house and unable to accept, is the same for women as for men, for which see " Men's Card Etiquette."

CARDS OF INTRODUCTION FOR MEN AND WOMEN.

A CARD with the name of its bearer written above that of the giver, prefixed by the word *Introducing*, is good form. This card is placed in an envelope addressed to the person to whom the introduction is made. On the lower left corner of the envelope is written, *Introducing Mr. or Mrs.* ——, with full name. This is left unsealed, and when presented or forwarded by post, the introduced person encloses his or her card, with present, also permanent, address written or engraved upon it. If the introduction is intended as a friendly one for both persons, a note of explanation may be sent by the person who introduces to the one to whom the presentation is made, which preparation is as discreet as it is courteous and kind, in most instances. Sometimes a card of introduction is asked of one who gives it reluctantly, and has not the courage to mention his or her unwillingness. Of course a person with delicate sensibilities or fine breeding will never ask for a presentation to another by note or card, but will leave this kindness to the impulses of the person who is able, but perhaps disinclined, to give it. Of course the latter is easily made aware of an opportunity to make two persons acquainted by card, and therefore such introductions should always be voluntary. If between friend and friend, the bearer of a card really asks for a hospitality that oftener than not is a courtesy for the one who sends the card, and not at all for the bearer of it. To present such a card is too often an implied request for attentions or hospitalities that cannot easily be refused, however untimely the demand may be.

A former free and easy, if not indiscriminate, habit of giving, and indeed of asking for, cards and letters of introduction, has fallen into disrepute, and very properly.

If there is a reasonable expectation of mutual benefit or pleasure, there need be no hesitation in offering a card that shall make two persons acquainted ; because in the give-and-take of society, if a blunder or misjudgment has been made by the person attempting to bring two people into a liking for each other, there are many not discourteous ways for an early conclusion of all knowledge of each other.

WHEN a *musicale*, high tea, or a party is given to or for distinguished persons, whether in the afternoon or evening, it is customary to send out cards engraved especially for this occasion, a visiting card not being sufficiently formal or complimentary. If it be a *musicale*, the word *Music* is usually engraved in the lower left-hand corner of an invitation, and the following is an approved form if it be in the afternoon. If in the evening, the invitation is issued by both husband and wife.

Mrs. John Herbert Jamison

At Home,

Tuesday, January tenth, from

four to seven o'clock.

Music.   10 *Porter Place.*

The word *Music* is omitted when there is to be an afternoon dance, and *Dancing* is substituted. This explanation is preparatory, and should for obvious reasons be included. It is not bad form to omit the word *Music* even when it is to be provided, a pleasant surprise adding much to the success of an entertainment.

If a reception of ceremony is given in honor of another, an engraved card has two approved forms of about equal acceptability. One is thus:

Mr. & Mrs. George William Taft

request the pleasure of

. . . .

company on Monday evening,

January tenth, at nine o'clock,

to meet

The Hon. Kenneth Colby,

Minister to France.

R. S. V. P.   *15 Oak Street.*

Another form of invitation has no blank space in which to write the name or names of expected guests, their address upon its envelope being regarded a sufficiently explicit mention of those bidden. It is engraved thus :

Mr. & Mrs. George William Taft

request the pleasure of your company

On Monday evening, January tenth, at nine o'clock,

to meet

Mr. & Mrs. Peter Howe Sinclair,

of Washington.

R. S. V. P. *15 Oak Street.*

Slight variations of these forms, such as breaking the lines into shorter lengths, and sometimes adding

the residence at the centre of the card, are about all
the differences a prevailing taste permits in cards or
notes of invitation to formal receptions that are given
in honor of friends or distinguished persons. They are
issued from ten to fifteen days in advance of the date
upon them, and it is not a little humiliating to thorough-bred and punctilious persons that abbreviations,
suggesting a reply to any formal invitation, should be
necessary. It is hoped and expected that they may be
safely dropped from cards before the termination of
this century. Of course, a reply is returned at once.

ETIQUETTE OF WEDDING CARDS.

THESE are furnished by those who give the wedding, and are sent out in the name of the bride's parents, guardians, or nearest kindred. The hostess requests the groom to give her a list of the names and addresses of such friends or acquaintances as he desires to invite to the ceremony only, and another one of those whom he wishes to see at the wedding reception, also; and she attends to this formality, or hospitality, in his stead.

Invitations to marriages are issued about two weeks before the wedding, although three weeks are preferred in circles where there is a pressure of social engagements.

If it is a house wedding there are usually two sets of invitations;—a *note sheet* for the marriage, which of course includes the reception, and another, a *card* for the reception. The following is the most approved formula for wedding invitations :

Mr. & Mrs. Franklin Hitt

request your presence

at the marriage of their daughter,

Grace Mary,

to

Mr. Joseph Henry Dorr,

Saturday morning, May tenth,

at twelve o'clock,

St. Agnes Church,

Tremont Avenue & 31st Street.

A parent does not mention a daughter with the prefix of Miss ; but if a guardian or other friend orders the invitations engraved, Miss cannot properly be omitted. A card of moderately large size with the following upon it is in good form :

Reception

from half-past twelve

until three o'clock.

38 *Clark Street.*

Sometimes this card is engraved in three lines instead of four, but this can be neatly done only when the hours are not divided, the reception or the marriage always being on the half-hour, to allow sufficient intervening time for driving home.

If the marriage is one that is likely to interest an uninvited public, a little card of admission to the church is a necessity, or a crowd of curious strangers might fill it to the exclusion of bidden guests. This card, also, is enclosed in the note of invitation and is presented to an usher at the church entrance. It is, also, given out to dependents and such other persons as are interested in the marriage. An approved form of admission card to a church wedding is thus engraved :

Please present this card at

St. Agnes Church,

Saturday, May tenth,

at twelve o'clock.

This card is much smaller in size than the reception card; but its lettering is the same script, without flourishes, and of small, but not very small size.

When a marriage ceremony is to be private, the family and near kindred are bidden verbally, as witnesses.

If a reception follows the ceremony, the invitation to the latter is thus arranged :

Mr. & Mrs. Kent Townsend

request the pleasure of your company

at the wedding reception of their daughter,

Elizabeth,

and

Mr. James Monroe Porter,

Monday evening, December fifteenth,

from half-past eight to ten o'clock.

202 Clover Avenue.

If there is no reception, or if there are many distant friends and acquaintances who could not be expected to make the journey even for a large wedding, an engraved announcement of it upon a note-sheet is prepared beforehand, in readiness to forward by mail the day after the marriage. The following is good form for such an announcement:

Mr. & Mrs. Franklin Hitt,

announce the marriage of their daughter,

Grace Mary,

to

Mr. Joseph Henry Dorr,

Saturday morning, May tenth,

Tremont Avenue & 31st Street.

A card or note of congratulation directed to those who announce a marriage, is *de rigueur* within ten days. An invitation to a wedding reception is accepted or declined within five days, provided there is an interval of three weeks, and within three days, if the marriage is but two weeks from date of invitation. Of course an acceptance or declination includes also a congratulation, and it is always directed to those in whose name the invitation is sent, and never to the bride or groom, even though one or both are the only persons known to those who are bidden. Of course, a special note may be written to the bride or groom.

DINNER CARDS OF INVITATION.

PERSONS who give many ceremonious dinners some-times order cards of invitation with blanks left for the insertion by pen of the names of guests, and also dates of dinners. The day of the week is added by the engraver, provided the hosts, as is usual, have an espe-cial one for all their ordinary dinner-giving. If they are to give an especially formal entertainment in honor of strangers, the card is engraved for this occasion, and includes the names of those for whom it is given. A permanent card may be engraved in good form, thus :

Mr. & Mrs. Harold Falk Green

request the pleasure of

. . . . . .

company at dinner on Thursday,

. . . . *at seven o'clock,*

11 *Gore Street.*

Those who have an especial veneration for persons of rank or high degree issue a note-sheet engraved thus :

To meet

PRESIDENT AND MRS. LINCOLN.

Mr. & Mrs. Hampton Gould

request the honor

of . . . . company

at dinner,

on Monday, April fifth,

at eight o'clock.

15 Spruce Street.

If another guest of less social distinction is included in the same honor, his name is engraved in smaller size on the line below, with *and* placed in the middle of the page between the two lines.

If it is a dinner in honor of a newly wedded pair or a friend who is of the same social grade as themselves, as most Americans reject distinctions, the names of the hosts are placed first, as in an invitation to a wedding or to a formal reception.

Replies to dinner invitations are sent on the day of their arrival. Even the slightest known possibility of a future detention compels all well-bred persons to refuse at once, and thus permit a host to fill their places at table.

CARDS FOR BALLS.

NOTE-SHEETS are used for private balls, and the engraved invitation is in the same form as for any evening party, except that its receiving hour is later, usually being 9:30 o'clock. *Dancing at eleven* is engraved upon the lower left-hand corner, and the invitations are issued two weeks, at the very least, in advance of the ball. Such invitations are accepted or declined within three days of their arrival.

LUNCHEON INVITATIONS.

Those who often entertain at mid-day, have a card engraved for this purpose. If it always is used for the same day of the week, the name of this day is also engraved, thus:

.

Mrs. James Keene Platt

requests the pleasure of your company

at luncheon,

on Friday, ... *at half-past one o'clock.*

R. S. V. P.   *4 Garden Street.*

A breakfast invitation is engraved in the same manner. Many entertainers, finding this form of hospitality less interrupting to other occupations or interests, vary the hour from ten to twelve o'clock, according to the time of year and the reason for it.

If either luncheon or breakfast is in honor of an especial guest, his name is engraved upon the card as for a reception, and *to meet* precedes it.

Breakfasts oftener include, or are given especially for men, than is the case with luncheons. At the latter, ladies only, as a rule, are present.

Suppers are seldom, if ever, so formal as to require an engraved card, except when given in honor of scientists, in which case the card, or note-sheet, is engraved in a form similar to that of one for a ceremonious reception.

For a golden or a silver wedding, it is considered in the best form to print the script in ink, as for other invitations ; but united monograms in gold or silver, as well as the two dates flanking them, in rather large, and perhaps ornamental numerals, are arranged across the top of the note-sheet. The engraving is thus for a golden wedding :

1840.   Monogram.   *1890.*

Mr. & Mrs. Matthew Tyne Ford,

At Home

Thursday, May fourteenth,

from four until six,

and from eight until ten o'clock.

For a silver wedding the hours are more indifferent to the possible weariness of age, and, as a rule the company is bidden to come at eight o'clock, and no concluding hour for the reception is mentioned. It is in good form to engrave *No presents*, in the lower left corner of such cards.

Responses with congratulations are sent at once.

DIRECTING CARDS.

ONE card or note is placed in the envelope that is directed, for example, to *Mr. & Mrs. Charles Henry Brown.* If their eldest daughter has been in society not more than two seasons, her name may be written beneath that of her parents upon the envelope. If she has been out a longer time, or there is more than one daughter in society, a second envelope, enclosing a card, is addressed to *Miss*, or *The Misses Brown*, and both cards are enclosed in an outer envelope and directed to the father at his residence. The mother accepts or declines at once. It would be in bad form to send social notes to a man's office.

Sons have separate cards addressed to their homes, or, if they have a club address engraved or written upon cards left upon those who direct invitations to them, of course a club is the place to which all their notes are sent. They reply for themselves at an early date.

Exceptional occasions require exceptional cards, and for such there can be no fixed etiquette. Refined tastes and an intelligence of the best social usages may be trusted as guides to good form in such cases.